The Hotel in Amsterdam

John Osborne's plays include: *Look Back in Anger* (1956), *Luther* (1961), *Inadmissible Evidence* (1965) and *A Patriot for Me* (1966). His collected prose, *Damn You, England*, was published in 1994 and the two volumes of his autobiography, *A Better Class of Person* (1929–1956) and *Almost a Gentleman* (1955–1966) were published in 1981 and 1991 respectively. John Osborne was born in 1929 and died at Christmas 1994.

by the same author

stage plays

THE ENTERTAINER

INADMISSIBLE EVIDENCE

LOOK BACK IN ANGER

A PATRIOT FOR ME

LUTHER

collections

JOHN OSBORNE: PLAYS ONE

(*Look Back in Anger*, *Epitaph for George Dillon*, *The World of Paul Slickey*, *Déjàvu*)

JOHN OSBORNE: PLAYS TWO

(*The Entertainer*, *The Hotel in Amsterdam*, *West of Suez*, *Time Present*)

JOHN OSBORNE: PLAYS THREE

(*A Patriot for Me*, *Luther*, *Inadmissible Evidence*)

collected prose

DAMN YOU, ENGLAND

autobiography

LOOKING BACK – NEVER EXPLAIN, NEVER APOLOGISE

(*A Better Class of Person* and *Almost a Gentleman*)

JOHN OSBORNE

The Hotel in Amsterdam

faber and faber

This edition first published in 2003
by Faber and Faber Limited
3 Queen Square London WCIN 3AU
Published in the United States by Faber and Faber Inc.
an affiliate of Farrar, Straus and Giroux LLC, New York

First published in 1968
by Faber and Faber Limited
3 Queen Square London WCIN 3AU

Typeset by Country Setting, Kingsdown, Kent CT14 8ES
Printed in England by Mackays of Chatham plc, Chatham, Kent

A CIP record for this book
is available from the British Library

ISBN 0-571-22190-4

2 4 6 8 10 9 7 5 3 1

The Hotel in Amsterdam was first presented at the Royal Court Theatre, London, on 3 July 1968. This production transferred to the New Theatre on 6 September and to the Duke of York's Theatre on 12 December 1968. The cast was as follows:

Hotel Porter Anthony Douse
Gus Joss Ackland
Laurie Paul Scofield
Margaret Isabel Dean
Annie Judy Parfitt
Amy Susan Engel
Dan David Burke
Waiter Ralph Watson
Gillian Claire Davidson

In the production at the Duke of York's Theatre, the part of Laurie was taken over by Kenneth Haigh.

Directed by Anthony Page
Designed by Tony Abbott and Donald Taylor
Costumes by Ruth Myers
Lighting by Andy Phillips

The Hotel in Amsterdam was revived at the Donmar Warehouse, London, on 11 September 2003. The cast was as follows:

Hotel Porter Alex Beckett
Gus Anthony Calf
Laurie Tom Hollander
Margaret Susannah Harker
Annie Olivia Williams
Amy Selina Griffiths
Dan Adrian Bower
Waiter Darri Ingolfsso
Gillian Laura Howard

Director Robert Lefevre
Designer Liz Ascroft
Lighting Designer Mick Hughes

Characters

Hotel Porter

Laurie

Margaret

Annie

Gus

Amy

Dan

Gillian

Waiter

THE HOTEL IN AMSTERDAM

Act One

The drawing room of a suite in a large, first-class hotel in Amsterdam. It is a fairly cheerful room as such hotel rooms go, with bright prints, plenty of low lamps and furnished in a rather friendly combination of thirtyish and tactful Hotel Empire. Three separate bedrooms lead off. The door to the hotel corridor opens and a Porter enters with a trolley filled with luggage. He is followed rather tentatively by three couples: Laurie and Margaret; Gus and Annie; and Dan and Amy. They are all fairly attractively dressed and near or around forty but none middle-aged. In fact, they are pretty flash and vigorous-looking. Perhaps Gus and Margaret less so than the others. This is partly because he is dressed a bit more conservatively than the other two men and she is visibly pregnant, though not unattractive. The Porter looks for instructions about the baggage. He looks for the leader and decides on Gus.

Porter Sir?

Gus I'm sorry?

Laurie I think it's the baggage, Gus.

Gus Oh.

Margaret Well, tell him, darling.

Gus No, it's all right. Now, let's see.

Annie Well, don't let's make an operation out of it. Those are ours. There, porter. Those two.

Porter Yes, ah but where are we all going to go? We don't, I mean we haven't had a look yet.

Laurie Why don't we sort them out and decide afterwards?

Margaret Brilliant.

Annie Some men are brilliant, aren't they?

Amy Can I help?

Margaret No. Gus can manage.

Gus Yes. Well it's just a question of sorting out the rooms, isn't it? They're all there.

Annie I should hope so. We're paying enough for them.

Margaret Well, don't let him stand there, darling.

Gus Well, we think we'll have a look at the rooms first and then decide where we're all going and –

Annie That'll take hours with Gus.

Margaret No. It won't. Look, porter, just put them all down on the floor and we'll sort them out ourselves.

Porter Yes, madam.

Gus Oh, do you think we should?

Laurie Yes, much quicker.

Gus We'll have to carry it.

Laurie That's true. I want a drink really. Have you got any –

Gus What – a drink? No, but we can order some now.

Laurie No. You know. Change. Tip.

Gus Oh, no, no I haven't. Let's see. No, I used it on the taxi.

Laurie Darling?

Margaret You know I haven't.

Annie I might have. Did you forget, Laurie?

Margaret Of course he didn't. He just didn't like to ask.

Annie Why on earth not?

Margaret He's terrified no one's going to speak English.

Annie You don't think they're going to speak Dutch, do you?

Laurie I suppose not. She's quite right though. I just feel I ought to and then I dry up. France is worst because it really seems so thick not to.

Dan Like Americans.

Laurie Exactly. And they're so foul, the French I mean. If you do have a bit of a go, they despise you and pretend they don't know. A waiter in Paris actually corrected me saying Vodka once. After all, that's a Russian word.

Annie I shouldn't let it worry you.

Laurie Well, it does.

Annie Gus is very good. Bit slow, but you're full of initiative always, aren't you, darling?

Gus Yes, I don't think I have that trouble so much. You can usually get someone to understand – especially nowadays.

Laurie That's the trouble. Amy, what should we give?

Gus I looked up the exchange.

Amy Here.

She tips the Porter, who looks neither pleased nor displeased.

Annie Thank heavens. Now Laurie can breathe and we can look around.

Laurie Just a minute. Do we all want a drink?

Margaret You mean: you do.

Gus I don't know. Do we, darling?

Annie You bet. After that journey. Aeroplanes!

Gus Margaret?

Margaret No. I'm not.

Gus Of course. Would you like something else?

Margaret Just mineral water. Perrier. Something.

Gus Amy?

Laurie I know Amy will and Dan's tongue's dropping out.

Margaret You hope.

Laurie I can see it from here. Why don't we –

Margaret No. It's too expensive.

Laurie But we ought to celebrate getting here. After all, we're all in one piece, we're all together, we've escaped and –

Annie Nobody knows we're here.

Laurie No one. Absolutely no one.

Margaret Well, that's not true.

Laurie (*to Porter*) Don't go. Well, no one who matters or will let on. Amy saw to that, didn't you?

Annie Oh, come on, let's order. I'll have a whisky sour.

Laurie Oh, isn't that going to be difficult?

Annie Difficult? A whisky sour?

Laurie If we all have something different –

Gus I see what he means.

Dan Yes. Reinforcements.

Laurie Perhaps we could vote on it. All the same thing.

Annie I *have* voted. I'm not being democratic just for convenience.

Laurie What about the rest. Amy?

Amy I really don't mind.

Laurie Good girl. And Dan, you'll drink anything. Right? Scotch?

Dan OK.

Laurie Right, then so will I. Gus?

Gus All right. But don't forget Margaret's Perrier.

Laurie Shall I?

Annie We would like one whisky sour, one Perrier water, a bottle of J. & B. or Cutty Sark. Some ice and some soda. (*to Laurie*) Happy?

Laurie Make it two bottles, we'll need them.

Annie And quickly please, if you can.

Porter Yes, sir.

Gus Well now.

Annie Let's look at the room. All right, Margaret?

Margaret Fine. Right.

Annie You have first pick.

Gus Oh, yes.

Annie I don't mind. As long as the bed's big and comfortable.

Laurie I do.

Margaret You would: spoiled.

Laurie Well, let's get it over.

Margaret Don't fret, darling. Your drink will be here soon.

Laurie God, I hate travelling.

Margaret Well, you've arrived. Relax.

Laurie Yes, that's true, isn't it? I suppose we really have. What a relief. All those passports and tickets and airport buses and being bossed about. Air hostesses – I'd love to rape an air hostess.

Gus Really? I don't mean about air hostesses. I rather enjoy all that travel guff.

Dan You would. Public school.

Margaret Now then, Dan, don't be chippy. You're very lucky to be with your betters.

Dan I know it. I hate the working classes. That's why I got out.

Amy You can never get out.

Dan I did. They're an unlovable, whining, blackmailing shower.

Annie What's he talking about?

Margaret Just being chippy.

Laurie Don't keep saying that. You should see my horrible family.

Margaret I have and now you're both being chippy.

Laurie We're both just saying we've got horrible families and that you're lucky to have nice, gentle, civilised, moderate parents like yours. Right, Dan?

Dan Right.

Margaret Oh, my goodness, class solidarity. Anyway, my mother's not that hot.

Laurie She's divine.

Margaret Well, you think so. She's just dull and sporty.

Laurie She's not. She's extremely attractive and intelligent.

Dan Not like my mum – scheming old turd.

Laurie And your mum's so ugly.

Dan Telling me.

Laurie Funny really, because you're not.

Annie He's beautiful.

Laurie Mine's got a very mean little face. Celebrates every effect, plays up all the time, to the gallery, do anything for anything. Self-involved, bullying.

Margaret Oh, come off it.

Laurie I suppose you think her face is pitted by the cares of working-class life and bringing up her sons on National Assistance. Well, it isn't. She has that face there because there's a mean, grudging, grasping nature behind it.

Margaret I don't know why nice men don't like their mothers.

Annie Gus likes his.

Laurie That's because she's probably nice.

Annie She isn't bad.

Gus No. I suppose she isn't, really.

Laurie And he's a bit queer too, remember.

Annie That's true.

Margaret But you always say you are a bit.

Laurie So I am. But not as much as Gus.

Amy What about Dan?

Laurie Well – either less than Gus or me. Or much more. He's more elusive. I mean Gus is so obvious. Those clothes. That's real conservatism.

Gus Are they awful?

Margaret You look dishy.

Laurie I think my mother *would* have put me off women for life. I mean just to think of swimming about inside that repulsive thing for nine months.

Margaret Please.

Laurie But I think when I was quite young I must have decided she was nothing to do with women at all. That's why the real thing was such an eternal surprise.

Margaret She'd love this. You usually butter her up.

Laurie She doesn't give a twopenny fart. Excuse me – I think I'm going to . . . It's the idea of my mother. Don't worry, I'll tell her before she dies. No. I die. She'll outlive me for years.

Dan My mother would have made a good air hostess.

Laurie Your mother! Listen, my mother should have been Chief Stewardess on Monster's Airlines. She'd have kept you waiting in every bus, withheld information and liquor, snapped at you, and smirked at you meaninglessly or simply just ignored you.

Dan Have you ever thought of airlines for homosexuals?

Laurie I say: what a splendid idea. You could call it El Fag Airlines.

Annie Gus could be a stewardess.

Laurie We'd design him a divine outfit. I say, I feel better already.

Margaret Don't get carried away. The holiday's only just started.

Laurie The great escape, you mean.

Gus You mean all the aircrew would be chaps?

Dan *And* the passengers.

Laurie Why don't we start it? Fly El Fag. The airline that floats just for HIM!

Gus It's not bad is it? I say, we're getting our wind back, aren't we? Just starting to feel safe I suppose.

Dan We're really here.

Laurie Really here.

Annie I don't know who's more astonished that we've all scarpered. Us, or whether *he* will be.

Amy K. L. will be *pretty* astonished when he finds out.

Margaret Let's face it: so are we.

Annie We do sound a bit amazed at our own naughtiness.

Laurie No, we're not.

Margaret Yes, we are. Come on. You are.

Laurie No, we are relieved, unburdened, we've managed to slough off that monster for a few days. We have escaped, we deserve it, after all this time. Just to be somewhere he doesn't know where any of us are. Can't get near us, call us, ring us, come round, write. Nothing. Nix. For a few blessed days. No K. L. in our lives.

Margaret You make it more cowardly than it is.

Laurie So what if it is?

Annie No. It isn't. We all deserve to escape. After all, he is the biggest, most poisonous, voracious, Machiavellian dinosaur in movies. And we all know what that means.

Laurie Quite.

Annie Sorry, Amy. I know he's your boss.

Dan He seems to be everybody's boss.

Amy Poor Dan.

Annie Yes. Married to the boss's secretary. That's probably the worst position of all.

Margaret You and I are in the same position.

Gus I suppose we all play different roles to the dinosaur. But they're still roles.

Dan Amy adores him.

Annie So does everybody. I do. And Margaret does. Gus can't live without him. And Laurie tries to pretend he can.

Laurie I can.

Annie I wonder if you will.

Laurie I have before and it sure didn't kill me.

Margaret I don't think I could bear any more recriminations.

Annie But the rest of us are still supposed to be friends.

Gus It's difficult, isn't it? Perhaps Laurie can come to some understanding.

Laurie Not this time, buddy, he's had it.

Gus I don't know how we'll cope when we get back.

Annie Darling. We've only just arrived.

Margaret How amused he'd be. Here we are congratulating ourselves on escaping from him and we've hardly stopped talking about him since we left Liverpool Street.

Laurie I wouldn't feel flattered to hear *what* we've said.

Annie He'd be amused certainly.

Laurie Amy, you are sure?

Amy Absolutely sure.

Laurie It would be great if he suddenly walked through that door while we were laughing and joking all together.

Amy He won't.

Gus What a thought.

Margaret Poor Amy. She's the real Judas amongst us. After all she is his secretary. *We're* conspirators.

Laurie I don't see that she's been disloyal. So what if she has! That cock's crowed a bit too often for every one of us. *And* everyone else. Those he's victimised at one time or another. Oh, he'll find another spare eunuch knocking around London. The world's full of hustlers and victims all beavering away to be pressed into K. L.'s service. Someone always wants to be useful or flattered or gulled or just plain whipped slowly to death or cast out into the knacker's yard by King Sham. Well, let him go ahead and get himself crucified this time. I know him not.

Annie What do you mean?

Laurie What I say.

Margaret He won't.

Gus Won't what?

Laurie Get himself crucified.

Gus No, I suppose not.

Annie No.

Dan Pity.

Amy He'll be all right. He'll find someone.

Gus I say, do you know we haven't looked at the view yet. It's rather good.

Margaret So it is.

Amy We're really here.

Dan I wish you'd stop saying that. Of course we're here. You made all the superb arrangements, didn't you?

Margaret Yes, thanks, Amy.

Laurie Hear, hear. Thank you, Amy.

Annie Well, screw the view, we haven't looked at the rooms yet.

Margaret Yes, we must do that now.

Annie Won't K. L. be furious when he can't get hold of you over the weekend? He knows you never go away.

Amy I said I was staying with some relatives in Yorkshire.

Annie But you're a hopeless liar. You're so transparent.

Amy I hinted it was really a lover.

Laurie Oh, he'd like that. More demolition around the joint.

Amy Yes, he was rather intrigued. So he didn't ask any questions.

Margaret Not even where to get hold of you?

Amy I said there was no phone. But I'd ring him.

Margaret Then won't you have to?

Amy Well, of course, he'll be furious when I don't. I'll have to say I wasn't well.

Laurie That won't wash. He'll ring Dan to stir it up.

Amy I don't think he'd do that. He wouldn't want to mess things up if he really thinks I've got a lover and Dan doesn't know about it.

Annie Don't fancy your first morning back, with your shorthand pad, when your boss has been deprived and rejected of men all weekend and you not on the phone having a bit on the side and not even confiding in him. He'll be *very* hurt.

Amy Oh, dear. Yes. He will.

Laurie So what. Say you had the curse and it ruined the entire rendezvous. That would appeal to him.

Amy Wouldn't wash. He knows my calendar better than I do.

Dan Knows your miserable little face, you mean.

Margaret Aren't they charming?

Annie Did you know that air hostesses have holy travail with the curse?

Laurie Really? Good.

Annie Seriously. To do with the air pressure or something.

Laurie Good. Jolly good!

Annie Either don't get it for months on end and worry themselves to death in case they're up the spout . . .

Laurie Fancy a pregnant air hostess. Think how high and mighty she'd be. Putting her feet up and pecking at all the customers' canapés.

Annie Or they get it twice a week.

Dan Do you mind. I feel a pain coming on.

Annie Wish you did. Then you wouldn't jeer at poor little Amy when she's boo-hooing all over K. L.'s office.

Dan Thank God they don't have women pilots.

Gus The Russians do.

Laurie Remember: never travel on Russky Airlines. Keep to El Fag.

Dan Or you might go up front and see a little bundle of Russian misery crying its eyes out over the controls.

Laurie All misted up and locking herself in the loo. Worse than seeing a little yellow face turn round and grin at you.

Annie Like the Lost Horizon.

Laurie Our bloody drinks are lost. Where is that hopeless Hollander? Do you suppose he understood us?

Margaret Of course he understood us. This isn't Bournemouth.

Knock. Waiter enters.

Gus Ah. There we are. Good evening.

Waiter Good evening, sir.

Margaret Now you can relax.

Gus I say, this is Haig. Didn't you order –

Laurie Doesn't matter. It'll take hours. You know what –

Gus Sure?

Laurie Sure. Open it, please, would you?

Waiter Yes, sir.

Gus I'm sure he'd change it if we ask him.

Margaret Laurie would die. Of embarrassment apart from anything else.

Laurie It's all right, leave it. I'll do it.

Waiter One whisky sour.

Annie Thank God for that. Thank you.

Gus That's all for the moment. Oh – Perrier? Yes. Here you are, Margaret.

Waiter Thank you, sir. Good evening.

Gus Good evening.

Waiter goes out.

Dan I don't think he approved of us much.

Laurie Did you think so? Yes. I had that feeling.

Margaret Thinks we're alcoholics.

Laurie I thought he thought the girls were probably OK. But not us.

Annie Perhaps he thinks we're none of us married.

Gus Oh, yes – having a real mucky weekend, gang bang stuff.

Laurie He looked very suspiciously at you.

Gus Did you think so?

Laurie I noticed it. Thought you were a bit effeminate I expect.

Gus Perhaps he did. I think it's these bloody trousers, darling. You said I should throw them away. They don't do much for me, do they?

Laurie Nothing desirable.

Annie Darling, you always look rather effeminate. You and Laurie both do. In different ways.

Gus Ah, but Laurie carries it off somehow. I don't.

Margaret Especially to foreigners.

Annie It's part of your masculine charm.

Gus What do you mean?

Annie Oh, I don't know. A kind of mature softness.

Margaret And peacockery.

Annie Yes, a bit uneasy sometimes but gallant and four-square all the same.

Laurie Doesn't sound too bad.

Annie It's lovely.

Gus You're quite right. I know foreigners think like that. It's hell when I'm in America.

Laurie They think I'm Oscar Wilde. It's very flattering.

Margaret And don't you play up to it!

Laurie Well, I mean you just have to, don't you? It's like they expect to see the Changing of the Guard.

Annie Thank heavens for the charm and femininity of the English male I say.

Laurie Well, American women certainly don't have it. Poor sods.

Margaret I'll drink to that.

Laurie Perrier. Ugh!

Margaret I like it.

Laurie Everyone's glass charged? Right . . . Well, here we all are.

Annie Here we all are.

Laurie Here's to all of us. All friends and all together.

Margaret Well, naturally.

Laurie No, it's not natural. It's bloody unnatural. How often do you get six people as different as we all are still all together all friends and who all love each other. After all the things that have happened to us. Like success to some extent, making money – some of us. It's not bad.

Gus Bloody good.

Laurie Everyone's married couples nowadays. Thank heaven we're not that.

Margaret You're drunk already.

Laurie You know what I mean.

Margaret Yes.

Laurie To us, and may the Good Lord bless and keep us.

All To us.

Laurie And preserve us from that dinosaur film producer.

Annie I don't think I can quite drink to that.

Gus It's a problem.

Laurie Well, suit yourselves . . . Ah, that's better.

Gus Isn't it good?

Laurie All right, Amy?

Amy Fine.

Annie Guilty?

Amy No. I'm forgetting it until Monday.

Annie I wonder if you will.

Laurie Well, give her a chance. Dan?

Dan Smashing.

Annie You know what: I think people who need people are the ghastliest people in the world.

Laurie Absolutely. We all just happened to find one another. At the right time.

Annie It sounds a bit Jewish showbiz.

Laurie I thought it was a rather tense Anglo-Saxon sentiment myself. I mean you couldn't sing it.

Annie Well, you could. It would be rather mediocre.

Laurie I mean you couldn't belt out a rather halting little comment like that. It's not poetic. It's just a smallish statement. About six unusually pleasing people. Well, five. God, I'm getting fat.

Margaret You've always been fat.

Laurie Really? *Have* I? I've deceived myself.

Margaret You're very attractive. Pleasing.

Laurie More pleasing than K. L.?

Margaret Yes. Don't know about more attractive.

Laurie Hell!

Amy We really *are* lucky. I mean it's a splendid hotel and a lovely suite.

Dan Which *you* can't afford.

Laurie You don't have to. *I* can. So can Gus. You made all the arrangements. And Dan's going to do all the talking.

Amy I think they all speak English.

Laurie You must admit it's better than that rotten Paris.

Annie I suppose we're all what's called spoiled.

Laurie What do you mean: spoiled?

Annie Well, first-class hotels, great suites, anything we want to drink.

Laurie What's spoiled about that? I'm certainly not spoiled. I work my drawers off and get written off twice a year as not fulfilling my early promise by some philistine squirt drumming up copy, someone who's got as much idea of the creative process as Dan's mother and mine rolled into one lazy-minded lump of misery who ever battened off the honest efforts of others.

Annie Writers are born to be reviled.

Laurie No they're not. They sit in judgement on themselves all the time without calling in outside help. They need to be loved and cared for and given money.

Annie We all love you and you make lots of money.

Laurie Where would K. L. be without me – where *will* he be without me to write his lousy pictures? Pretty all right, I guess. And without Gus to edit them into making sense and cover up his howlers? Of course, I suppose you'll go on doing it.

Pause.

Well, not this one. Besides, he hates it if I make money. I think he tips off the tax man. We don't live in Switzerland any of us, do we? More sense but still . . . Loaded with distinction and not a CBE to go round. When I think of the rotten dollars I've made –

Margaret Don't.

Annie And K. L.

Laurie Well, lolly doesn't worry him. He spends it. You just round up a few people like Gus and me here, turn them up on the gas and if you suck around the blood counter at the supermarket long enough, you've produced another picture. And you go on doing. What I do, I get out of the air. Even if it's not so hot always, I put my little hand out there in that void, there, empty air. Look at it. It's like being a bleeding conjuror with no white tie and tails. Air . . .

Margaret Hot.

Laurie It never pays what it costs . . . No. I'm feeling quite relaxed now. Sure you won't drink?

Margaret I do keep telling you.

Laurie Sorry. Actually, I do speak Italian quite beautifully, don't I, darling?

Margaret The accent's good.

Laurie Poor vocabulary. But they don't mind if you make it up. They love it. (*all very fast but clear*) Prego, prego. Si, grazie. Signorina. E machina bella. Grande film con regissori K. L. con attrici Inglesi tutte bellissima. Attrici Inglesi molto ravissante crumpetto di monde. Per che. Me Lauri scritori Inglesi famioso connossori, grosso. Molto experementi, senza pommodori, si. Oggi declarimento attrice Inglesi crumpetto elegante, insatiabile, splendido lasagne verde antifascisti pesce Anna Magnani Visconti arrivederci con rubato grazie mille, grazie. There, wasn't that good! Allemange basta! Pasta per tute populo. Kosygin pappa mio. Si grappa, per favore.

Margaret I think I'm going to sort the rooms out.

Laurie Oh, leave it.

Margaret I want to unpack.

Laurie Oh, all right.

Margaret And I expect the others do. Unless they want an Italian lesson.

Laurie Shall we go to an Italian restaurant tonight?

Gus That sounds good. Darling?

Annie Perhaps we should try the local hostelries.

Laurie Yes. I expect you're right. I'm too fat for wop food.

Margaret Dutch food's rather heavy.

Gus Enormous portions. Good beer. I've got an information thing here.

Annie Oh heavens – don't start on that already.

Gus Well, we'll have to make a decision.

Laurie I don't see –

Gus Might have to book a table or something. If we want to get somewhere good.

Laurie Yes, I see.

Annie You both make it sound so difficult.

Laurie My dear Annie, it is difficult. I can't think of anything that comes easily. It's all difficult.

Annie You need one of those things that fortifies the over forties.

Laurie I'm not over forty!

Margaret Well, you look it.

Laurie What are you trying to do to me?

Margaret No, you don't. You look like a teenager.

Laurie Yes, a plump, middle-aged, played-out grotesque.

Annie Never believe in mirrors or newspapers.

Laurie I thought I'd got the mirror fixed . . . I need another one after that.

Margaret Come on, let's explore this place and see what we've got for our money. Annie?

Annie follows her. Also Gus, who looks helpful.

Laurie Over forties. I heard a disc jockey the other day introducing a pop version of 'Roses of Picardy'. 'Picardy,' he said. 'Where's that?' Help . . .

Dan Do you ever look to see if your birthday's listed in *The Times*?

Laurie Always.

Dan And is it?

Laurie They missed me out the year before last. Seemed like an obituary only no notice. When you do something, try to do something, take a look at someone else's efforts, you ask yourself, *I* ask myself, is there something there that wasn't there before? Well . . . I picked this damned paper up and it seemed I hadn't even been born any more . . . Do you ever have a little lace curtain in front of your eyes? Like little spermy tadpoles paddling across your eyeballs? No? Do you think it's drink or eyesight?

Dan Drink.

Amy You ought to watch that.

Laurie I've been watching it for years. Fascinating. And tell me, do you ever either of you, no you wouldn't, Amy, but you, Dan, do you ever wake up with your fingertips all tingly and aching?

Dan No.

Laurie Well, do you ever wake up with an awful burn in the stomach?

Amy Yes, he often does.

Laurie And then what do you do?

Dan Get up. Work. Paint if it's light.

Laurie This is about five o'clock is it?

Dan Usually.

Laurie And you can actually work, can you?

Dan Not always.

Laurie Do you wake up, Amy?

Amy I usually wake up.

Laurie And then?

Amy I make coffee or give him a glass of milk.

Laurie And have a bit of chatter?

Dan That's it. Until it's time for her to get off to K. L.

Laurie I'm afraid I usually need a drink. It's the only thing that burns it out. Need to weld my guts with a torch. Then about nine, it eases off. I read the post. Try to put off work. Have a so-called business lunch. That's a good waste of time. Then I know I'll have to sleep in the afternoon.

Amy Does Margaret get up when you're like that?

Laurie She can't – poor old thing. You see she can't get off to sleep. So by the time I'm about to totter about downstairs, reading last night's evening papers, she's only just managed to get off. Especially now.

Amy When she's pregnant?

Laurie motions her silent at the word.

Laurie So, I'm afraid we're a bit out of step with sleep. When I was eighteen I used to sleep fourteen hours on Sundays. When my mother would let me.

Dan My mother made too much noise.

Laurie If *only* you can find enough energy. Where do you find it? Where's the spring?

Amy You're loaded with it. You've got far more than Dan.

Laurie No, I haven't. Dan doesn't need energy. He runs perfectly efficiently on paraffin oil. You fill him up once a year and he's alight for another twelve months. With me, I need the super quality high-thing stuff poured into my tank twice a day. Look at K. L. He's unstoppable, you never have to wind him up. He just goes. Like that.

Amy He gets very worn out.

Laurie I should think he does. If I did what he does in a day, I'd be in bed for a month.

Dan He delegates.

Laurie Ah, yes – the operator's alchemy. Where do you get it? He takes it from us. We could be giving it to one another. He's been draining our tanks, filling his own. Filling up on all of us, splitting us up.

Margaret, Annie and Gus return.

Margaret Give what to each other?

Laurie A little vitality.

Annie We're all right. And we're on hols. So we can recharge.

Laurie Yes, we've got away.

Annie The rooms are fine. You and Margaret are having that one. Gus and I this one and we decided Amy and Dan would like that one with the view. It's nice.

Amy Are you sure?

Annie They're all nice. Now we can get our stuff in.

Margaret Gus has done nearly all of it already. Gus, you are a darling. Honestly, you two! Letting Gus do all the carrying.

Laurie Good for his figure.

Margaret Typical.

Laurie And bad for my kidneys.

Margaret Are you going to help me unpack?

Laurie Do you want me to?

Margaret No. I don't think so.

Laurie I can.

Margaret I don't doubt it.

Laurie Shall I talk to you while you do it?

Margaret No. Talk to Dan and Gus. I might lie down for a bit.

Laurie Let me –

Margaret Please stay where you are.

Annie Ours won't take a second.

Laurie You seem to have brought an awful lot of stuff. What are you going to do? Play golf? Hunt or something?

Annie Mostly Gus's stuff. Medicines, all chemist's counter.

Dan Got my easel?

Amy Yes.

Dan Right. Just in case.

Annie and Margaret go to rooms.

I'll never use it.

Laurie Working on your own. I could never live on my own. Oh, I have done. It's been all right for a time. But what about now and then, the steep drop and no one there. And no one to phone or too far away.

Dan Or too early in the morning.

Laurie That's one of the few good things about movies. You do work with others. Bit like the army.

Gus I suppose we really have made the right selection? Over the rooms?

Laurie Who cares? They'll all be the same.

Gus I just thought Margaret ought to have a nice one. If she's not sleeping.

Laurie Gus, I know you mean well but please forget about it. I say, old Amy won't get the sack when she gets back to K. L.?

Dan No. He relies on her too much.

Laurie Do you mind?

Dan Mind?

Laurie I shouldn't think you see much of her. His nibs keeps her at it. Seven days a week.

Dan He pays her well. More than I earn. It works out.

Gus Don't think that would suit me.

Dan Annie can't see all that much of you.

Gus Oh, a fair bit. He tries to keep me away from her, mind you. You know: don't bother to drive home. Stay here and we can make an early start at breakfast. But I hardly ever do. I need a bit of looking after, I'm afraid. I hate staying in other people's houses. Unprepared and all that. No shaving stuff. Or someone else's. And I don't like really sleeping on my own. Somehow, well the quality of sleep is different. Do you know what I mean?

Dan I can sleep anywhere.

Laurie I think I know. More drink – before they come back?

Gus Well. It does seem a bit unfair to drink so much in front of Margaret.

Laurie It isn't. But just don't say so.

Gus Oh? All right. Well, here's to all of us. Amsterdam . . . What a brilliant idea of yours. He'd never think of here.

Laurie No?

Gus Not exactly his sort of place I'd have thought. Not much night life.

Dan Few bank managers dancing with each other and that's it.

Margaret (*off*) Laurie. Would you ring down for some more Perrier for me?

Laurie OK, darling.

He hesitates, looks hopefully at Gus, who responds.

Gus I'll do it.

Laurie (*grateful*) Oh, would you? Thanks. (*He pours out for Dan.*)

Gus (*on phone*) This is room 320. Yes. Oh, yes – room service, please . . . Hullo, can I have two large bottles of Perrier water? And, oh yes, some ice. And a bottle of Cutty Sark. You brought Haig last time. Yes. Thank you. All fixed.

Laurie Thanks. And no one's to buy an English newspaper. Right?

Dan Right. It's not your birthday, is it?

Laurie I wonder why she didn't ring down herself.

Gus Unpacking, I suppose . . .

Dan I was thinking the other day: do you think they make bicycle clips any more?

Laurie Hadn't thought of that. No, of course. All those little bare black ankles.

Gus Bicycle clips . . . I think I've still got mine.

Laurie Like Picardy I should think. No one would know. Like those things you used to wear on your sleeves.

Dan I should hope not.

Laurie Well, of course, I never did. I'll bet you did.

Gus What?

Laurie Wear those things. Up here.

Gus No – I don't think so.

Laurie Do you have one of those little pocket diaries? You know, for appointments and things.

Gus Yes.

Dan No.

Laurie Well then, Gus. I wonder if this happens to you. You know how just after Christmas and you've got nothing to do except feel ill and miserable and dread those last days of December? If you haven't got to hell out of it. Well, I always start my new diary off before the New Year. Put my licence number in it because I can't remember it. Why *should* I remember it? Then you put in your telephone numbers – I even put my own in. Otherwise I might ring one I had years ago . . . Well, and then there are the names of all those people, not *all* those people but some people, because I don't keep many in there and then you know – every year I sit down and there's not just one I don't put in again, there's four, five, six. I think there are only about eleven in this year – and that includes people like you and Dan and K. L. *He'll* be out next year. And my agent. And that's about it. Oh, and my mother . . . Hey, what are you all doing in there?

Annie (*off*) Unpacking!

Margaret (*off*) What do you think?

Laurie Well, come back in.

Amy Coming!

Laurie Margaret! We're all missing you. We're on our own.

Margaret (*off*) No, you're not. You're getting stewed.

Laurie We're six and there are only three in here.

Annie Bad luck.

Laurie We love you. Why have you gone and left us? We came here to be together. And you all disappear off to the bedroom or the bathroom and dolly about with your rollies and skin tonic. Come back in here! You're needed!

Gus Yes, come back. Annie!

Annie (*off*) I'm unpacking all your laxatives and pouve juices.

Amy (*appearing*) All done! It's a lovely room, Dan. Go and look at the view.

Dan I will.

Laurie You deserve a lovely room, my dear. Come here and give me a kiss. Just for arranging everything if for nothing else ever. Not a hitch.

Amy It was easy. K. L.'s got a good travel agent.

Laurie You didn't use *him*!

Amy He won't let on. I briefed him.

Laurie Good girl. Well, if you lose your job, you'll have to come and work for me. Have a drink. Won't be as exciting as K. L. But you'll get more time off.

Knock on door.

That's him. He's found out where we are. You've bungled it and he got on a plane and did it the quick way.

Amy Come in.

Laurie Scusi, scusi. Momento, momento, tutte in bagno. Basta, per favore.

Waiter enters.

Waiter Whisky sour?

Laurie No, Cutty Sark.

Amy Annie, did you order a whisky sour?

Annie (*off*) Yes. I knew you'd all forget me.

Gus Why didn't you tell me? I've ordered.

Annie (*entering from bedroom*) Easier. Thank you.

Gus I ordered. Cutty Sark. And Perrier. And ice. You won't forget!

Waiter Very well, sir. (*Goes.*)

Gus Crossed lines. All right, darling?

Annie Everything's out. Anything from bowels to athlete's foot.

Laurie Do you know there really is such a thing as writer's cramp?

Annie Sounds rather comic – like housemaid's knee.

Laurie Not funny if you're a housemaid or a writer.

Dan Have you had it?

Laurie Naturally. What's more I get psychosomatic writer's cramp.

Amy You can type. I've seen you.

Laurie The commitment's too immediate. Horrifying. Like kissing someone for the first time and then bingo you're having to slap the breath of life into some rotten little fig of a human being that heaved its way between you five seconds afterwards. Do painters get anything like housemaids?

Annie Aching backs, I suppose, on murals and things. Do you?

Dan Not much.

Laurie That's because you work at a controlled pace, you see. Everything you do has rhythm, you see. Systematic, consistent. *That's* the thing. Mine's all over the place.

Annie You produce the goods.

Laurie Are – but do I then?

Annie Don't fish. You know you do.

Laurie But what goods? I ask myself: can anything manufactured out of this chaos and rapacious timidity and scolding carry-on really *be* the goods? Should it not be, I ask myself. What do I ask myself? Perhaps I shouldn't be rhetorical and clutter conversations with what-do-I-ask-myselfs? Won't the goods be shown up by the way of the manner of their manufacture? How can they become aloof, materials shaped with precision, design, logical detail, cunning, formality? And so on and so on.

Annie And so on. You're not such a bad tailor.

Laurie No, I'm not.

Annie There, you *were* fishing.

Laurie *And* I provide my own cloth. Any clunkhead can cut. I don't mean in your sense, Gus.

Gus What? Oh, no – you're right.

Annie I've a feeling we're getting back to K. L. *You* said let's leave him behind. But you won't.

Amy He will.

Gus Well, it is difficult, you must admit. He rather makes one talk about him.

Annie Perhaps we should go straight back to London and be with him after all.

Gus Don't suppose he'd have us all together.

Annie Why were you doing your parliamo Italiano bit?

Amy He thought it was K. L.

Annie *That* would have fooled him!

Gus You didn't really, did you?

Laurie No. Except with him nothing is so awful he couldn't visit it on you.

Annie No one would think you'd been loving friends for ten years.

Laurie You can't be loving friends with a dinosaur.

Annie What are you then?

Laurie A mouse – what else?

Annie Some mouse. With the soul of a tiger.

Laurie A mouse. With the soul of a toothless bear.

Annie What's Gus?

Laurie Gus? He's a walking, talking, living dolphin.

Annie Amy?

Laurie An un-neurotic fallow deer.

Annie And Dan?

Laurie Dan, he's a bit difficult. Rather cool, absent-minded but observant. Orang-utan.

Annie You're a rather sophisticated mole who keeps pushing up the earth to contract all her chums in the right place at the right time.

Amy And Margaret – what's she?

Laurie Don't know. That's a difficult one.

Gus Something frightfully attractive but efficient.

Laurie A rather earnest chimpanzee. Practical, full of initiative.

Annie Inquisitive?

Gus I don't think chimpanzees are very attractive.

Annie Neither are moles.

Laurie Oh, yes they are. I'd love a mole for Christmas. Perhaps you can buy rubber ones in Amsterdam.

Dan I don't think orang-utans and what was it, fallow deer, are very well matched myself. It's the sort of thing a marriage-bureau computer would come up with.

Annie I don't think he was very good at all.

Laurie Dinosaur was good.

Gus That was easy.

Annie And you didn't characterise your dinosaur.

Laurie I will.

Annie Don't. We know.

Laurie Perhaps he's not the same dinosaur to all of us. It's obvious, but it may be his little tiny dinosaur's trade trick.

Margaret enters.

Margaret Was that the waiter?

Gus Wrong order. Your Perrier's coming.

Margaret You rang down?

Laurie Yes. We did.

Margaret We?

Laurie Gus did. It's the waiter – he likes rough trade, don't you, Gus?

Gus grins.

It's the beatings at that prep school and scrumming down in the mud and being genuinely liked by the men, no?

Gus I don't think the waiter's exactly my dish. But I quite like the Dutch I think. Seem rather nice up to now.

Annie We've not taken much of a sample. Taxi drivers, receptionists . . .

Laurie Air hostesses. International. But I think we're going to like the Dutch. I think we're going to have a lot of time for the Dutch, as my horrible mother says.

Annie Only means nasty contraceptives to me. And chocolate.

Laurie What, you mean chocolate-coated ones? Oh, I see. Talking about that arse-aching subject, somebody told me only very bovine girls can munch away at 'em. Air hostesses are made for the pill, for instance. Will you have a pill with your coffee, madam, with the airline's compliments? *They* take them. If you've any temperament at all, you just kick around in your stall like a racehorse. I mean you couldn't *give* the pill to racehorses.

Dan Well, it would be doping them, wouldn't it?

Gus I say, this is good, isn't it.

Annie Don't say it – we're really here.

Laurie Well, we are.

Knock at door.

Annie Come in.

Waiter comes in.

(*to Laurie*) Sorry. I thought we'd had enough of your Italiansprache.

Gus Ah! Good evening. (*as if he hadn't seen the Waiter before*)

Waiter Sir. (*He puts things down.*)

Pause.

Gus Where would you recommend us all to eat on our first night in Amsterdam?

Waiter It depends on what you have in mind.

Gus Well, what we have in mind is absolutely the best, not necessarily the most expensive or the most famous. I mean: what would you suggest?

Waiter It's difficult, sir. There are many excellent places to dine.

Amy I've got a typed list here, Gus. More or less in order.

Gus I just thought he might –

Laurie I should forget it.

Gus What?

Laurie Amy's well trained. She always gets out a list of the six supposed best restaurants for K. L. I've often wondered what he'd have done if his surname had been Youn or Yeo or Yarrow.

Gus Why?

Laurie We'd have called him K. Y.

Annie You would.

Gus What's K. Y.?

Laurie Gosh, these prep schools were tough, weren't they? Or did you use Matron's Vaseline? You do like it rough.

Gus Oh!

Waiter goes out.

Laurie Oh. You know what its legitimate, well-intended use is? Cleaning surgical instruments. Well, you remember that assistant K. L. had a couple of years ago . . .

Annie What happened to him?

Laurie Stepped on the trapdoor in front of the desk one day I suppose. Anyway . . .

Margaret I don't remember him.

Laurie Yes, you do. English faggot he picked up in Hollywood. About thirty-five, all tight pants and white socks and greying hair.

Margaret Oh,. and that expression . . .

Laurie Yes, I think you called him the Frozen Madonna. I called him Sibyl. He had a crown of sibillants over his head. He sounded like a walking snake pit. I mean, you could even hear him from one end of the Crush Bar at Covent Garden to the other – *packed*. So, Sibyl told me he went into this chemist and there was this other faggot behind the counter. He says, very dignified: can I have a tube of K.Y. please? The assistant doesn't say a word, wraps up package, gives it to him. Then, as he drops his change into his palm, he says . . . 'Have fun.' And Sibyl said, 'I looked and said, "What? Cleaning my surgical instrument?"'

Margaret Now, listen, I think Gus is quite right, we should have a talk about what we're going to do and then make a decision.

Annie That could take hours.

Margaret Well, it mustn't. This is our first evening. We've made all this effort to get here and go through all these elaborate conspiracies not to let K. L. know where we are. Amy may have lost her job. *And* we haven't got all that much time.

Laurie I wonder where we'll all sit down and do this again.

Annie If you'd said 'when' I'd have belted you.

Gus Tomorrow. Tomorrow.

Margaret Oh, come on. Amy, let's look at your list. I don't think we want to go anywhere too ambitious tonight.

Gus All right, Margaret?

Margaret I just think we've been travelling and getting out of London and we should go somewhere fairly quiet but very nice and – oh, I don't know. What have we got here . . . ?

Gus We must go to the Rijksmuseum.

Margaret Yes, Gus, but not tonight. Rembrandts are for the morning.

Annie And there's the Stedelijk.

Dan And those Indonesian places where you get thirty great dishes.

Amy You're greedy.

Margaret This sounds the sort of thing: fairly conservative but attractive seventeenth-century surroundings, beautiful tables and candles. That sounds like us. Tonight anyway. Laurie, choose.

Laurie They all sound good. Like the waiter said. That one you said looks pretty good.

Margaret Annie?

Annie Yes. That sounds what we'd like. Gus doesn't like too much noise. He can't talk *and* eat.

Dan Anything will do us.

Margaret Right. Then let's get the concierge to book a table. As there's six of us. And it may be busy.

Laurie I'm on holiday, Amy will do it.

Margaret We're all on holiday. Why should she do it?

Amy I'll go and ring down. Give me the list. (*Goes off to bedroom.*)

Gus Then we'd better talk about tomorrow. What people want to do. I mean, some may just want to sleep or do nothing.

Margaret No. I don't think that's right. We should try and all do the same thing. Unless . . . Well, we'll see what everyone says.

Annie I can tell you what everyone will do – just talk. About what to do, where to go, what we should wear to do it. And we'll end up getting drunk at lunchtime in the American Bar and eating in the Hotel Dining Room.

Laurie Sounds delightful.

Gus I suppose it isn't very adventurous.

Margaret Annie, you'll have to help me.

Laurie We're here – that's adventurous.

Annie We'll talk about tomorrow over dinner.

Gus I'll bring my guide.

Margaret Amy!

Amy Yes?

Margaret I know nobody knows we're here but we might get one call for this room. If we do it'll be for me. Perhaps you should tell them. Save confusion.

Laurie For you! But we agreed not to tell *anyone* we were here. Except the blooming nanny and she wouldn't get through. Who did you tell, for God's sake?

Margaret Gillian.

Laurie What did you go and tell your bloody sister we were here for?

Margaret Oh, don't be silly. I told her not to tell anyone we're here.

Laurie But what did you tell her for? She's not one of us.

Margaret Isn't she?

Laurie Well. she's not really anything to do with K. L. And besides, she wouldn't like it. She thinks we're all a bit flippant and middle-aged. Not half as middle-aged as her.

Margaret Come on. You like her. It's just that she's been having a bad time lately.

Laurie What bad time?

Margaret I'm not sure. But this affair she's having –

Laurie Oh, fleecing another rich duke of £500 and clenching her fists because she didn't lose her cherry until she was twenty-eight and she doesn't think she gives satisfaction and she plays Bach fugues all night and doesn't wash her hair because it's all so difficult. Blimey! I think *I* complain. She needs public recognition for the suffering she undergoes, that's all. Then she'll feel better. She should get the Golden Sanitary Towel Award. K. L. can give it to her at the Dorchester with all the past winners present.

Margaret Well, I told her if things got too bad to ring me.

Laurie You didn't say she could come here?

Margaret I said if things got too much for her, I'd get her a room.

Laurie Oh, lovely for your friends.

Margaret I don't think anyone will mind.

Laurie Did you ask them?

Margaret You don't have to ask friends everything.

Laurie Perhaps you do. If she comes out, we can all go home. Why don't she and K. L. get together?

Margaret She's my sister, Laurie. I'm not having anything happen to her. Just for want of a phone call.

Laurie She won't do anything to herself. Not till it's too late. Like getting laid.

Margaret I love her.

Laurie You can. Don't expect your friends to.

Gus Poor girl. What is it?

Laurie She's just a star wrecker of other people's coveted, innocent little weekends, that's all.

Gus Oh, if she turns up, we'll look after her. She can't spoil anything. It's all right.

Annie Of course it is. I know how to deal with Gillian. Put her to bed, that's the best thing.

Laurie It's a long way to come to go to bed. I mean, I know people go to New York for haircuts –

Margaret Let's not argue, darling. I'm sure it won't happen. She doesn't want to worry me.

Laurie She wants to worry everybody.

Annie Listen, Laurie, darling. We're together. We've got days ahead. No one knows where we are. Except your daft nanny. Now –

Gus She's right. Oh, I'm sure that restaurant's first class and tomorrow we'll do just as we like and go round the

Leidseplein and Rembrandtsplein and the discotheques and clubs . . .

Annie Drink up, Laurie. You'll feel better.

Laurie I shall, I shall. I feel better already.

Gus Old K. L. wouldn't like this at all. He'd have wanted to be out on the streets by now. Not just sitting around talking. What would he do?

Annie Oh, exhaust a list three times as long as Amy's in half the time. Play games into the night. Games with victims.

Gus I mean he'd hate this. Just us: talking among ourselves.

Laurie Well, as we're all here because of him, because of him, let's drink to him. Don't go yet, Amy. Ladies and gentlemen, to our absent friend.

Margaret What's the time?

Amy Six o'clock.

Gus He must have rung somebody by now.

Margaret Perhaps we should have a little zizz before we go out to dinner.

Annie Good idea.

Gus He may not know we're *all* gone yet.

Laurie Not together, anyway.

Annie I should think he'll go off to Paris or something. Anything. And when we get back just manage to make us feel foolish. We'll just say we went away for the weekend. Do we have to tell him everything? What am I saying?

Margaret What about Amy?

Annie That's up to her.

Laurie Oh, he'll be adroit. But he'll also be maladroit. He won't be able to resist trying to discover where we've been and who with.

Annie Perhaps he just won't care. As you said, it's not exactly his idea of fun. God, he'd be pleased and amused.

Laurie Oh, he'll appear to be innocent, rational, ill-used. Slightly impatient.

Gus The trouble is he creates excitement.

Laurie Not half enough.

Gus Perhaps we're all second rate and need second-rate excitement, sort of heats one's inadequacies.

Laurie He takes nothing out of the air round *his* head. Only us. Insinuates his grit into all the available oysters. And if ever any tiny pearls should appear from these tight, invaded creatures, he whips off with them, appropriates them and strings them together for his own necklace. And the pearls have to be switched or changed about. Otherwise the trick, the oyster-rustling, would be transparent and the last thing he wants made known is his own function or how he goes about it. Where does he get the damned energy and duplicity? Where? He's tried to split us up but here we are in Amsterdam. He has made himself the endless object of speculation. Useful to him but humiliating for us. Well, no more, my friend. We will no longer be useful to you and be put up and put down. We deserve a little better, not much but better. We have been your friends. Your stock-in-trade is marked down *and* your blackmailing sneering, your callousness, your malingering, your emotional gun-slinging, your shooting in the dark places of affection. You trade on the forbearance, kindliness and talent of your friends. Go on, go on playing the big market of all those meretricious ambition hankers, plodding hirelings, grafters and intriguers. I simply hope tonight that you are alone – I know you won't be. But I hope, at least, you will feel alone, alone as I feel it, as we all in our time feel it, without burdening our friends. I hope the GPO telephone system is collapsed, that your chauffeur is dead and the housekeeper drunk and that there isn't one con-man, camp follower, eunuch, pimp, mercenary, or procurer of all things possible or one globe-trotting bum boy at your side to pour you a drink on this dark January evening . . .

Annie Well – Amen.

Gus Gosh – it's started to snow.

Laurie I think I'm the only one who believed all that. Good, all the better. We can get snowed up.

Margaret Well, I'm going to have a zizz.

Gus Yes. I should. And we can discuss the alts later.

Laurie Oh, yes we'll discuss them.

Margaret Laurie?

Laurie Just finish this.

Margaret We don't want to go out too late.

Amy I'll book the table.

They go to their rooms.

Annie Think I'll have one too.

Laurie Finish your drink first. I am glad it's snowing. How I hate holidays. Those endless, clouded days by the pool even when it's blazing sun. Do you remember doing it? All together – at K. L.'s villa? We drank everything you could think of from breakfast onwards after that vile French coffee. The deadly chink of ice in steaming glasses all day. Luxury, spoiled people. Lounging together, basting themselves with comfort, staring into pools. A swimming pool is a terrible thing to look into on a holiday. It's no past and no future. You can stare into a stream or a river or a ditch. Who wouldn't rather die in a ditch than in a pool? I'm too fat for pools and the pretty girls with their straps down and their long legs just make me long for something quite different. I always want someone to write me long, exhilarating love-letters when I lie there with the others . . . A handwritten envelope by your towel, curling up.

Gus We didn't get on too well that time, did we? I'm sure it wasn't our fault.

Annie We played too many games – too many bloody games, expected too much of the sun and each other and disappointed K. L. . . .

Gus He asked us all again.

Laurie Yes. I read somewhere that one of those communications people, the men who tell you what it is we're all feeling now because of *the* media, said that marriage and romanticism was out. At least with the young people.

Annie I suppose it was on the way out when we came in.

Laurie I wonder where we ought to go to live. All those sleepy-eyed young mice squealing love, love. Scudding into one another, crawling over each other, eyes too weak for bright light, tongues lapping softly . . . all for love, a boy's tail here, a girl's tail there, litters of them.

Dan Think I'll take a look at my things. (*He goes out.*)

Gus Is he all right?

Annie Yes. You know Dan.

Laurie I think he may be a very violent man.

Gus Dan?

Laurie Fools make him suffer. So he paints or reads a book.

Annie Or goes into his fallow deer.

Laurie Don't blame him.

Gus Well, perhaps you'd better come with your whatever-I-was.

Annie Yes.

Gus So, shall we say seven forty-five? First drink. Well, not first drink, really.

Laurie Nineteen-forty-five hours. First drink.

Gus Good. Where's my street guide? (*He goes.*)

Laurie Ought to have a bath, I suppose.

Annie Not sleepy?

Laurie Yes. I wish I could live alone. Do you?

Annie No. I never have.

Laurie I have sometimes. It can be all right for weeks on end even. But then. You have to crawl out of the well. Just a circle of light and your own voice and your own effort . . . People underestimate Gus I think.

Annie So do I.

Laurie Do you think *you* do?

Annie I don't think so.

Laurie He doesn't exhilarate you like K. L.?

Annie No.

Laurie No. Gus has created himself. Thinks he's nobody, thinks he behaves like it. Result: himself.

Annie Do you think Margaret's all right?

Laurie No.

Annie Can I do anything?

Laurie She doesn't like being pregnant.

Annie Who does? A few mooish ladies.

Laurie She feels invaded, distorted. About to be destroyed.

Annie Why do you both do it then? Was it the same with the others?

Laurie I thought we might get pleasure from it. She thought I would get pleasure.

Annie And you haven't?

Laurie Perhaps they're like holidays or hotels.

Annie No. Not hotels. You couldn't live without them.

Laurie I love Gus very much. I think he really believes most people are better than him . . . I only suspect it.

Annie He loves you.

Laurie Good. Try not to be too restless. Don't do that. What were we all doing this time last year? I mean were we all together or separate?

Annie Separate.

Laurie I wonder *what* we were doing. We'll have a good evening. I feel better already. The snow's stopped.

Annie Good. Seven forty-five then. Try and kip. (*She kisses him lightly.*)

Laurie I will. And you, Annie. And you.

She goes to her room, taking her handbag. The three doors are closed. Laurie looks out of the window.

Curtain.

Act Two

The same. Two evenings later. They are all in the sitting room, looking much more relaxed, enjoying the First Drink of the Evening.

Gus Well, what's the schedule for this evening?

Margaret I don't care.

Amy Neither do I. Everywhere's been good.

Laurie I know. Isn't it weird?

Annie Why shouldn't they be?

Gus Yes, well, if we came up with an absolute dud at this stage we could hardly complain.

Margaret I must say that list of yours has been infallible.

Laurie Brilliant.

Dan All smashing.

Gus Not a dud. I say, we really have had quite a time, haven't we? Friday evening seems weeks away. So does K. L. Right after the first evening. Not a foot wrong. We're jolly lucky.

Laurie I mean even that Indonesian place was quite funny.

Dan Actually, it was a 'lovely feast of colour'.

Margaret All those dishes. How many do you think we actually got through?

Amy I think Dan had a bit of the whole thirty or whatever it was.

Laurie Still looks as lean and clean as a brass rail.

Margaret And we got Laurie round to the Rijksmuseum, without too much bitterness.

Laurie I felt at home in all that non-conformist gothic.

Annie And there *were* the Rembrandts.

Laurie Yes. We needed a drink after that. I keep thinking of him watching his house being sold up. All those objects, all those pieces and possessions got with sweat, all going. K. L. would have enjoyed that.

Annie Don't be unfair.

Laurie And his child dead. What was his name? Titus?

Annie I liked the place with the bank managers dancing together.

Laurie That's because you danced with that chambermaid from Hanover.

Annie It seemed only fair. It's a bit churlish to just go and gawp like a tourist. I think you were very mean not to dance.

Laurie No one I fancied.

Margaret Annie's right. You got frightfully stuffy and absent-minded all of a sudden.

Laurie I was worried about you and that lady in the black dinner jacket.

Margaret You didn't show it. I don't know what I'd have done if Gus hadn't protected me.

Annie She really fancied you, didn't she?

Amy I'll say. I've never seen anything like it.

Dan She was just queer for pregnant girls.

Margaret I'd have thought that would have put her off.

Gus Not at all.

Annie What about tonight?

Gus Yes. We must make a decision.

Annie Where's the list, Amy?

Dan Let's have a look. What are the alts?

Gus We've still got lunch tomorrow.

Laurie Why don't we stay the extra day?

Annie We've done all that.

Margaret Yes. Amy must get back.

Laurie But why? I don't see it.

Margaret Because she doesn't want to lose her well-paid job, which she also likes.

Annie And she has obligations.

Laurie What obligations? You don't have obligations to monsters.

Dan What about this? I don't know . . .

Amy Why don't we go to the place we went to on the first evening?

Laurie That was wonderful.

Dan At least we know it's first rate.

Gus You don't think that's being a bit unadventurous, do you?

Annie Yes. Let's chance our arm.

Laurie Why should we?

Margaret I agree. We should try something different.

Dan What for? Not that I mind.

Laurie You girls are so ambitious. Even if it's for others.

Gus Really escaped, didn't we? I haven't laughed so much for months. Have you, darling? You said last night.

Laurie I still think we should go back a day later.

Margaret No.

Laurie Amy could fix it.

Amy Of course. Why don't you? I could go. It seems silly when you're having such fun. Dan, you could stay with them.

Annie I think we've voted on that one.

Laurie Oh no we haven't. I wonder when we'll all sit down like this again.

Margaret Damn it, we've done it enough times before.

Annie Sure, we'll do it again.

Laurie Yes. But when? How? Where? How do we arrange it? I don't want to go back to London.

Annie Who does?

Laurie No. I mean it. What is there there for any of us? We should all go and live together somewhere.

Margaret Where, for instance? Somewhere you didn't have to pick up the phone for room service.

Laurie We need a broken-down Victorian castle or something, oh, with all the plumbing and jazz we wanted. But lots of space around us. Acres of land around us, empty, chipped and scarred still by Roman legions.

Annie Sounds freezing.

Laurie What would you prefer, a sonic bang up your lush southern parkland? We could do what we liked, have lots of children.

Gus There aren't many of us.

Laurie We'll think of some others.

Annie But who?

Gus K. L. would find out about it.

Laurie Let him. You'd all come, wouldn't you?

Annie What about staff?

Margaret Good question.

Dan You'd need lots of nannies.

Laurie Yes. Well . . . we'd get ex-stewardesses from El Fag Airlines. They're absolutely wonderful nannies. Poor old things will work for absolutely nothing if you get a really rejected one.

Amy And the rest of the staff?

Laurie They must be people we know. People who'd fit in with everyone. I would learn carpentry. I've always wanted to do that. And bricklaying. I could work on the house. Gus knows all about electricity. Margaret could drive. Except we wouldn't use the car much. Annie's the great horse expert. We could use them and maybe hunt if we got over our green-belt-liberal principles. And Dan could, well, he could just paint.

Gus Who do we know?

Laurie Well, we ought to make a list. That's one thing, do you realise, we've escaped from, Margaret? My relatives and all those layabout people I pay to look after us. So that, the theory being, we are able to do other things, not bother with inessentials because we've *made* it.

Annie I thought your Nannie was good?

Margaret She's very good.

Laurie Only she doesn't look after *me*. She looks after two creatures who don't even know yet they're being waited on.

Annie I thought you didn't like being waited on.

Laurie I don't. But if I pay for it at home I expect it.

Amy They're only tiny babies.

Laurie Darling, don't say 'tiny babies'. All babies are tiny compared to people. Even if they had to be landed like killer sharks, they're still tiny. What I hate about them, it's like my relations and K. L., you always, you're expected to adjust to *their* mood, their convenience, their bad back, or I-don't-know-I'm-just-depressed. What are they going to be like when I ring the bell, when I open their letters? They never anticipate you.

Annie Gus never anticipates for himself.

Margaret How?

Annie He's always taken by surprise by situations and people's reactions.

Margaret Laurie rehearses them all.

Gus Am I?

Annie He was cutting some trees down just by the pond one day. And he'd keep stepping back. Just about a foot away from the pond. 'You will mind the pond,' I'd say to him. 'What? Oh. Yes.' Then he'd do it again. 'Don't forget the pond.' 'No . . . all right.' Always a bit surprised. I watched him for two days and then I thought I can't go on. I'll leave him to it. He missed it by inches for a whole morning. And then fell in.

Gus Yes. That's quite right. I did feel surprised when it happened.

Laurie The mistake is to feel guilty. That's always been my mistake. He's driving you about because you're cleverer than he is. And though I say it, he can't even drive as well as I can. That's why he's a servant, she says. Well, why can't he be a good one, I say. I wouldn't want him to wait on me. I don't know though. Why do it at all? There are third-rate servants. Perhaps I've got the ones I deserve, like the relatives I deserve.

Dan As the old saying goes, we're all bloody servants.

Laurie You're right. Deliver the goods, or the chopper. I suppose that's right. Do we deliver the goods?

Annie If someone's cooked you a meal decently and woken you and been able to smile as well, that would be delivering the goods.

Margaret It would.

Laurie Are we spoiled?

Annie Staying in a luxury hotel on the continent because you're afraid of your servants?

Laurie That does make it sound stupid. Very.

Gus But that wasn't the main reason.

Laurie Yes. I just send my nasty relations a cheque. I never see them. They certainly don't want to see me.

Dan What are they?

Laurie Retired, rotten, grafting publicans, shop assistants, ex-waitresses. They live on and on. Having hernias and arthritic hips and strokes. But they go on: writing poisonous letters to one another. Complaining and wheedling and paying off the same old scores with the same illiterate signs. 'Dear Laurie, thank you very kindly for the cheque. It was most welcome and I was able to get us one or two things we'd had to go without for quite some time, what with me having been off work all this time and the doctor sends me to the hospital twice a week. They tell me it's improving but I can't say I feel much improvement. How are you, old son? Old son? We saw your name in the paper about something you were doing the other day and the people next door said they thought you were on the telly one night but we didn't see it, and Rose won't buy the television papers so we always switch on to the same programme. Rose doesn't get any better, I'm afraid. I brought her a quarter-bottle the other day with your kind remittance which served to buck her up a bit. Your Auntie Grace wrote and said she'd heard Margaret was having another baby. That must be very nice for you both. We send our best wishes to you both and the other little ones. Hope you're all well. Must close now as I have to take down the front-room curtains and wash them as Rose can't do it any longer, but you know what she is. Bung-ho and all the very best. Excuse writing but my hand is still bad. Ever. Your Uncle Ted. P. S. Rose says Auntie Grace said something about a letter from your mother which she sent on but I'm afraid she sent it back unopened. She just refuses to pass any comment. She told me not to say anything about it to you but I thought I'd just – *PASS IT ON TO YOU?*' (*He gestures towards them.*) Pass *that* on!

Margaret Oh, don't talk about them. They're so depressing.

Annie They sound quite funny.

Laurie They're not quite funny, Annie. They're greedy, calculating, stupid and totally without questions.

Margaret They're just boring.

Laurie They're not that even. They're not even boring. Now I am boring. I am quite certainly the most boring man you have ever met in your lives. I see you're not going to contradict me so I won't let you.

Gus As a matter of fact, I was going to contradict you because I am infinitely more boring than you could ever be even on a bad day. Not that I think you could be even then.

Margaret You're both drunk.

Laurie No, we're not. At least Gus may be a bit. I am just straightforwardly boring. Look, some people when they're drunk are dreadfully boring, especially when they're supposed to be freewheeling and amusing. Now, drink doesn't do that to me. Drink doesn't change one, does it?

Annie Not much.

Laurie There you are. I am just as boring drunk as I am sober. There is no appreciable difference. If I could tell you, if I could, how much I bore myself. I am really fed up with the whole subject . . . I am a meagre, pilfering bore.

Dan Well, don't be a bore and enlarge on it any more.

Laurie You're drunk! (*Laughs.*) I say, Dan's drunk. We really are having a time . . .

Margaret Did you see Terry had married that girlfriend of K. L.'s?

Annie Yes.

Dan Not that horrible Tina Whatsaname?

Amy The same.

Laurie That's the movie business. Where the producer persuades the director to marry *his* crumpet.

Margaret He hasn't got a very strong character.

Laurie What does that mean?

Annie I think he'll survive her.

Laurie I mean K. L.'s got a *strong* character. Hasn't he? Does it mean simply someone who can impose their will on others? Can be politic and full of strategy!

Margaret You know what I mean about Terry.

Laurie I saw something very interesting the other day. No, somebody told me.

Amy About air hostesses?

Laurie No, about nurses. Is this boring? That's the window sign of a bore. He always says to you at some point, 'Is this boring?'

Annie Fascinating.

Laurie Yes, well, I think it probably is. Because it may affect us all in some way. Well, apparently if you've got the real incurables, the carcinoma or some dance like that going on inside you, the doctors very sensibly start pumping things into you at the right time and make you as thumpingly stupid as possible. Unfortunately, the nursing profession, being imperfect, like El Fag Airlines or any other concern, contains a considerable and dangerous fifth column of popish ladies in starched collars and cuffs who'll fail to give you your shot of blissful dope come six o'clock. Nothing to call on in the small house but a couple of codeine and an Irish lilt. So, do you know what they do, the clever ones, the doctors? Well, if they should decide they'd rather a patient didn't lie in agony, they insist on a roster of Australian nurses. They're the best. The Aussies. They'll give you enough for you and your horse if you tell 'em. So, if you ever wake up after you've been in hospital for a little while and one day a little cobber voice says to you, 'And how are we today, Mr so-and-so?' you know you've scored.

Annie Yes. That's better than the lady pilot.

Laurie Annie?

Annie What?

Laurie You're called Annie and I'm called Laurie.

Annie What are we supposed to do?

Margaret Hadn't you thought of it before?

Laurie No. Isn't that odd? Had you?

Gus Not me. I don't think. Annie mentioned it to me one day.

Laurie Dan?

Dan I've got used to it. The trouble with being spontaneous, or even trying to be, and I think one can, the trouble is it does put you at the mercy of others. That's not the same thing as being a bore.

Laurie What do we ever go back to England for? What do we do it for?

Annie I thought you never wanted to come away.

Laurie It's the bitchiest place on earth.

Margaret That's the name of the place you come from. Now, what have we decided?

Gus About what?

Laurie We haven't decided anything. Um? (*Holds her hand.*)

Margaret I mean where are we going for our last night?

Knock on door.

Laurie You didn't order anything, did you?

Gus No.

Amy Probably the maid with all those clean sheets for when we go.

Annie Come in.

The door handle rattles.

Gus No key. Well, if it's K. L., he's too late. We've done it.

He goes to the door, opens it. A girl of about thirty, Gillian.

Laurie Gillian.

Margaret Darling.

Gillian I'm sorry. I should have warned you.

Margaret (*to her*) My darling, what's the matter? You look ill.

Gillian I didn't have a chance. I'm all right. I couldn't remember how long you were staying.

Margaret Why didn't you ring me? Come in and sit down. Take your coat off.

Gillian No. I think I'll keep it on.

Laurie Oh, sit down and take the bloody thing off. It's hot in here.

Gillian I'm sorry. I should have rung first. I couldn't find the number.

Laurie Just the name of the hotel?

Margaret Laurie, give her a drink.

Gillian No, I'll have a Perrier.

Laurie Don't tell me *you're* pregnant.

Margaret Give her one.

Gillian Just a small one, very small.

Laurie Did you bring your own nose dropper?

Gillian Well, how are you? Have you had a good time?

Laurie Fanfuckingtastick! Never stopped laughing, have we?

Amy We've had a marvellous time. Why didn't you come?

Gus I think you'd have enjoyed it. We've done quite a lot in an easy sort of way, done what we wanted –

Laurie After discussion.

Gus After discussion. And all the places we've been to have been tremendous fun – thanks to Amy's list.

Dan I liked that place like the Brasserie at Joe Lyons where everyone sang 'Tipperary' – in English.

Gus Yes, I think you'd have liked it – don't you, darling?

Annie I don't think she'd have liked that place much, Margaret didn't.

Gus Oh well, Margaret didn't feel so hot for a while.

Margaret I just can't stand the smell of beer and all those awful swilling, ugly-looking people.

Annie I think the men enjoyed it rather more.

Amy I loved it.

Dan You even sang – as usual.

Laurie What do you mean – the men liked it?

Annie I mean you sometimes try and fumble your way back to childhood while we watch and get impatient and wait for you to stop.

Laurie Perhaps you should try coming along.

Annie Yes. We found two really remarkable restaurants, we discovered a new game, or rather Laurie invented one, and Gus had us in stitches telling us stories about his regiment in the war, with two versions to every story, one tragic and one comic, the tragic one always being comic and the comic one always tragic. Laurie's starting a new airline and Dan's putting out a new scent. They'll tell you.

Gillian I'd like to go to the Rijksmuseum.

Laurie There are other things here besides Rembrandt. We needed a drink after him. Drink?

Gillian Thanks.

Laurie Too much?

Gillian No, fine.

Laurie Only I don't want you leaving any because I'm an impoverished writer with a wife, children, useless servants, a family of ageless begging-letter writers, a trencherman nanny and three dogs as big as you. I haven't yet found my voice. I write too much not enough, I have no real popular appeal, I take an easy route to solutions –

Annie Stop being paranoid.

Laurie Why? If a man is ill he isn't a hypochondriac. And if he's attacked he's –

Margaret Oh, shut up, Laurie. Can't you see there's something the matter?

Laurie Who with? Annie?

Gillian I told you – honestly – everything's fine. I just thought I'd come suddenly.

Margaret Darling, I've known you all my life. Something's very wrong. Do you want to tell me?

Laurie Oh, leave her be.

Margaret I know her. You don't.

Gillian I wish I *had* come. You all look as if you've had a super time.

Laurie I'll bet we do – now. (*to Margaret*) You're right – it's not a very convincing performance.

Gillian Tell me what else you've been doing. It does sound good. I've always wanted to come to Amsterdam.

She leans forward avidly. The others decline visibly. She has broken the fragile spell.

Did you go on the canal?

Dan Yes.

Gillian And that modern art gallery, whatever it's called. Can't pronounce Dutch. And the harboar, or where is it, where all the tarts sit in the windows looking like dolls. This hotel looks splendid. They were terribly nice downstairs. They seemed to know all about you lot up here. They smiled the moment I said who I wanted. Do you think I can get a room? Perhaps I could get one down the hall. All I need is a little room. I suppose I could come in here with you most of the time. Don't let me interrupt what you're doing. I'll just finish this and change, I think. Perhaps I could have a bath in your room, Margaret, if Laurie doesn't mind. What time are you going out? I don't want to hold you up. I needn't unpack. Unless you're dressing up. I could change in your room though and see about the room later. Do you know where you're going tonight?

Gus We were – just discussing the alts. Perhaps we should go somewhere you'd like.

Gillian Don't change anything because of me. It's my fault for turning up like this. Just do what you would have done by yourselves. Please don't let me change anything . . .

Laurie Gillian, for Christ's sake burst into tears . . .

Slowly she crumples and they watch her.

Gillian Please . . . take no notice. I'll get a room down the hall.

Margaret pulls her arm around her and leads her into her bedroom and closes the door.

Laurie Drink anyone?

Annie Yes, please.

Gus Poor girl.

Dan Just as well we're going tomorrow.

Amy I wonder what it is.

Laurie Oh, either her lover's married and can't or won't get a divorce or he *isn't* married and she can't bring herself to offer herself up to something total. Variations on some crap like that. But I tell you, she's not going to blight our weekend. We've had ourselves something we want to have and we made it work and she's not going to walk in here on the last night and turn it all into a Golden Sanitary Towel Award presentation.

Annie I'm afraid she's done it.

Laurie Well, we mustn't let her. Look, Gus, flip through that list and we'll decide where to go and either she can come with us and put on a happy face or –

Annie Oh, not that.

Laurie No, I agree – the miserable one's better. You and Dan can talk to her a bit about the Rembrandts and painting and Dutch domestic architecture and what

Marshal McLuhan said to Lévi-Strauss while they were on the job. Otherwise, she can just shut up and leave us to it. Or Margaret can stay with her arms around her in the bedroom all evening.

Gus That's not very fair on poor old Margaret.

Laurie Her sister's not being very fair to us.

Annie That's not her fault.

Amy No. Dan will talk to her and cheer her up. He's good at that.

Laurie Why should he?

Dan Sure. I don't mind.

Annie Why should we? We do. Listen, Margaret will listen to her and calm her down. Then we'll take her out with us. She'll be all right.

Laurie But will we be? If I didn't know I'd think it was a last-minute joke of K. L.'s on us. Blimey, she's turned it into Agony Junction all right. Look at Gus. Dan, have some more in there.

Gus Oh, she's not such a bad girl.

Dan She's brought London with her . . .

Gus Perhaps we should go to the place we went on the first night, anyway.

Laurie I suppose so.

Gus I think she'd like it. It's quiet and the food – did you have those herrings?

Amy My chicken in that pastry thing was wild.

Laurie Oh, she'll be sick or pushing her food away or leaving it and pretending she's enjoying it and filling us up with guilt and damned responsibility. Damn her, we've just got together again, she's an odd man out, we haven't got time to take off for her coltish, barren, stiff-upper quivering lips and, and klart-on. Am I unsympathetic?

Annie Yes.

Laurie I'm sorry . . . all of you . . .

Dan Not your fault.

Gus Not anybody's fault.

Laurie Baudelaire said – can't remember now.

Gus Someone said the other day: 'What do you do if you live in San Francisco, you're twenty-one and you go bald . . .'

Laurie He said, I know, 'Beauty was something he only wanted to see once.'

Annie She's quite attractive.

Laurie Gillian?

Annie Um.

Gus Very.

Amy Not as much as Margaret.

Annie She's prettier than she thinks, that's the trouble.

Laurie She should take some pretty pills. So should I. I'm all water. Heavy. Bit of underwater fire like North Sea gas. Not much earth or air either . . . What a precious remark – that's her fault. Did I tell you about the boy with the crocodile shoes?

Annie No, but it's too long. I've heard it.

Dan Tell them the one about the nun in the enclosed order.

Gus Wish I could remember jokes.

Laurie Young nun enters an enclosed order with a strict vow of silence. The silence can only be broken once every three years with two words. So: after three years the girl goes to the Mother Superior, who says: 'Now my child, three years have passed since you entered the order. You have kept your vow of silence. It is now your privilege to say any two words you wish to me.' So the young nun pauses painfully, opens her mouth and says: 'Uncomfortable beds.' So the Mother Superior says, 'Right, my child, and now you may go back to your work.' Three more years pass and she comes before the Mother Superior again. 'You have observed the rule of this order for three more years. It is your privilege to say two words to me – if you wish.' So the nun hesitates and then says: 'Bad food.' 'Very well, go back to your work, my child.' Another three years pass and the nun is brought in front of the Mother Superior again. 'Well, my child, three more years have passed. Is there anything you wish to say to me?' The nun raises her eyes and, after an effort, she whispers: 'I want to go home.' 'Well,' says the Mother Superior, 'I'm *glad* to hear it. You've done nothing but bitch ever since you got here . . .'

Annie Why don't you go in and see how Margaret's managing?

Laurie I don't think I'm what's wanted in there. Margaret will call if she wants me.

Annie Are you sure?

Gus Shall I knock?

Laurie No, leave them. Did you like her, Amy?

Amy Gillian? I don't really know her. I felt sorry for her when she was sitting there trying not to spoil everything.

Laurie But doing it pretty well all the same.

Dan Why did you ask Amy?

Laurie Because Amy likes nearly everyone.

Annie You make her sound imperceptive, which she's not.

Laurie No. I think she is blessed with loving kindness

Dan So – we've decided on the first-night place? . . . Laurie?

Laurie What?

Annie Yes.

Gus Well, we thought so, Dan. Unless you'd like to suggest something else. We thought . . .

Annie Discussion.

Dan Perhaps we'd better start getting ready slowly. Amy?

Amy Yes. Right. Now.

Laurie You two really are a lecherous couple.

Amy Me?

Laurie Me? Yes, you two. You toddle off to the bedroom every evening twenty minutes before the rest of us.

Annie Good for them.

Laurie Perhaps you simply organise these things better. Is that it, Dan? I'd never thought of it before. Perhaps, working efficient secretaries make the ideal wives. I mean it does need fitting in with everything else. How long have you been married?

Amy Nine years.

Gus Marvellous. Is it really?

Annie Nine isn't so long. Some people have golden weddings.

Laurie Golden Sanitary Towel Weddings. I think Dan's pretty formidable. I bet if you looked at his sexual graph of desire his would be steady, unchanging, up there like Nelson on his column, and there'd be mine bumping about among the lions.

Dan Wish it were true.

Laurie Well, get along then.

Amy Actually, I wanted to write a couple of postcards.

Gus *Are* you? I don't think you should write postcards from here somehow. I haven't. Deliberately. It seemed like giving evidence that we'd ever been here, all of us.

Laurie Yes. Well, go and do it, whatever it is. Only don't keep us waiting.

Annie Oh, who kept who waiting last night?

Laurie I did.

Amy See you then.

Gus Seventeen-forty-five.

They go, closing the door behind them. Pause.

What'll you do when you get back?

Laurie Don't know.

Gus No, *we* weren't sure. Were we, darling?

Laurie I've tried not to think about it.

Gus Perhaps we should all have dinner the first night back. Where could we go?

Laurie I'll ask Margaret.

Gus That new place you took us to the other week was nice. I wonder if K. L. discovered it.

Laurie Hope not.

Annie I expect he has.

Gus I wonder if he'll ring when we get in.

Laurie Sure to.

Gus Perhaps he'll wait for one of us to ring him.

Laurie He can.

Gus Well, it worked . . . Are you going to work as soon as you get back?

Laurie If I can. You?

Gus I've got to. I should be there tomorrow really. Do you know what you're doing next weekend?

Laurie Margaret would know.

Gus Perhaps we could do something.

Laurie Maybe. We'll talk about it on the train . . .

Gus I think I'll go and have a bath. A *real* bath, I mean. What's the time? Yes, seventeen-forty-five. I'd better book the table, hadn't I? Best not disturb Dan.

Annie I'll have one after you.

Gus What?

Annie A bath, my darling.

Gus OK. Well, I'll have one first, then I'll run one for you and I can shave while you're in it.

Annie Right.

Gus You might as well stay and have another drink with old Laurie.

Laurie I'm all right. Perhaps she'd like a kip.

Annie Bit late now.

Gus Do you know what you're going to be wearing this evening?

Laurie No. Oh, the same as the first night I expect.

Gus Yes. I see. I remember. Only it helps me when I make up my mind what to put on. It's that chocolaty mohair kind of thing.

Laurie That's the one.

Gus That's good. Well, fine. See you then.

Annie And, darling – wear your purple tie.

Gus Are you sure?

Annie It suits you.

Gus Not too –?

Laurie Yes. Divine.

Gus Oh, all right. Annie gave me that. It's awfully pretty. She's got the most amazing flair and taste in things like men's clothes. In everything, come to that.

Laurie Except men.

Gus Yes. Well, blind spot in us all. I'll call you when I've run the bath, darling. And I'll put some of that oil in, shall I? If there's anything – with Gillian – you know, I can do, give a knock.

Laurie Go and have your bath. I want to see you properly turned out for our last night.

Gus Right.

He goes into his room and closes the door. Pause.

Annie Are you sure I shouldn't go in to Margaret? Girl stuff.

Laurie If you want to.

She doesn't move.

You haven't been married before, have you?

Annie No.

Laurie I have.

Annie It's quite a well-known fact.

Gus Yes. It's like having had a previous conviction

Annie Of course, I lived with people before Gus.

Laurie Many?

Annie I don't think so; some would. But I don't think it was inordinate – no. I lived with each one an inordinate time.

Laurie I wonder what my other wife thinks of me.

Annie Has she married again?

Laurie Twice. I wonder what my name even means to her.

Annie Ever see her?

Laurie No. I dread bumping into her somewhere. Even here the other night, I thought I saw her in that smart place.

Annie Why do you dread it?

Laurie I don't think she likes me.

Annie Why not?

Laurie I imagine I wasn't very kind to her.

Annie Weren't you?

Laurie I don't know. I wish I could really remember. I try to. I hope not. But I'm sure I was.

Annie It doesn't mean that *you're* unkind.

Laurie Doesn't it?

Annie Oh, come. Just capable of it. Like everyone.

Laurie Amy is never unkind.

Annie You don't want to be like Amy.

Laurie Don't I?

Annie No . . . It will be all right . . . when we get back.

Laurie Yes.

Annie Don't grieve.

Laurie Annie. Laurie. I do.

Annie I know.

Laurie You live with someone for five, six years. And you begin to feel you don't know them. Perhaps you didn't make the right kind of effort. You have to make choices, adjustments, you have requirements to answer. Then you see someone you love through other eyes. First, one pair of eyes. Then another and more. I was afraid to marry but afraid not to. You see, I'm not really promiscuous. I'm a moulting old bourgeois. I'm not very good at legerdemain affairs . . . Do you like Margaret?

Annie Yes . . . Have you been unfaithful to her?

Laurie Yes.

Annie Enjoyable?

Laurie Not very.

Annie Often?

Laurie No. Not inordinately.

Annie When was the last time?

Laurie Six months. Just a few times.

Annie Before that?

Laurie Not for ages.

Annie What's ages?

Laurie When she was in the nursing home . . .

Annie In the nursing home? You mean, not –

Laurie Yes.

Annie I see.

Laurie Are you shocked?

Annie No. Surprised . . . Not really.

Laurie I thought you might say: men!

Annie You're not men! I'd better go and change.

Laurie Gus'll call you. Have some more . . . I've wanted to tell you.

Annie Have you?

Laurie No one knows. You won't tell Gus, will you?

Annie I won't tell anyone . . . Why did you want to tell me?

Laurie Why? Because . . . to me . . . you have always been the most dashing . . . romantic . . . friendly . . . playful . . . loving. . . impetuous . . . larky . . . fearful . . . detached . . . constant . . . woman I have ever met . . . and I love you . . . I don't know how else one says it . . . one shouldn't. . . and I've always thought you felt . . . perhaps . . . the same about me.

Annie I do.

Laurie When we are all away – you are never out of my heart.

Annie Nor you out of mine.

Laurie So there it is. It's snowing again . . . I wonder what it'll be like in London.

Annie God knows.

Laurie If we were going by plane, I'd say perhaps it'll crash. Or we won't be able to take off.

Annie We'll have longer on the train together.

Laurie Together? Yes, and we can all get drunk on the boat.

Annie Perhaps we should change and go on the plane after all. I don't know that I can face the journey with you there . . . sorry. A touch of the Gillians.

Laurie A touch of the Annies.

Annie I love you . . . I can never tell you . . .

Laurie Thank you for saying it . . . Bless you, Amsterdam. Wouldn't K. L. be furious?

Annie Because it's happened or because he doesn't know?

Laurie Both.

Annie I think he'd be envious because it's happened. I fancy he's suspected for a long time.

Laurie Do you?

She nods.

Yes. He doesn't miss much. Do you think Margaret knows?

Annie I think she might. I would.

Laurie And Gus?

Annie No.

Laurie Good . . . I think we need another . . . (*He pours for them both. Looks down at her.*)

Annie Don't look at me.

Laurie I'm sorry. I shall never be able to come back to this place again.

Annie Which?

Laurie Both. The hotel. Amsterdam.

Margaret comes in.

Annie How is she?

Margaret Oh, she's a little better. Some of it came out and, oh dear, I don't know why some people's lives have to be difficult. I'll tell you about it later. Anyway, she's resting on our bed. I thought she might be able to have a little zizz and then, if she's all right, she can come out with us. If not, I'll stay in with her.

Annie But you can't do that. We must all go out, together, on our last night. You've got to.

Margaret Oh, we'll see. We'd better get her a room. Laurie, can you ring down and ask reception if there's a single room down the hall near us she can have?

Laurie OK. Like some Perrier?

Margaret No, thank you, Laurie, are you all right?

Laurie Fine.

Margaret No, you're not, I can see. He doesn't look well. Does he, Annie?

Annie I think he's just getting a bit seasick already.

Margaret It's not that. Even Laurie waits till the same day.

Laurie Who is it this time?

Margaret What? Oh, Gillian. It's too complicated, now.

Laurie Nothing's too complicated now.

Margaret Darling,. I think you started drinking too early. You started right after breakfast . . . Oh, yes, she saw K. L.

Laurie Saw him. How?

Margaret He asked her round for a drink.

Laurie When was this?

Margaret Friday.

Laurie I never thought he'd ring *her*. She didn't tell him where we'd gone?

Margaret Yes, Laurie, I'm afraid she did.

Laurie She did! The stupid, dopey mare!

Margaret Oh, stop it, Laurie. It doesn't really matter, as it's turned out. He didn't ring or *anything*, did he?

Laurie You mean she told him the hotel, the lot?

Margaret You know how clever he is at winkling these things out of people. She said he seemed so concerned about us all, and she was, oh, distraught about her own weekend. He managed to convince her that we'd really want him to know.

Laurie Don't tell me she's having an affair with him. They deserve each other. Except he'd spit her out in one bite.

Margaret Listen, Laurie, I'm worried about that girl. She's my sister and I love her, and I think she came very close to doing something to herself this weekend.

Laurie Don't you believe it. She just models for it. People like her don't go home and do it. They choose a weekend when there's someone likely to come in the flat or they don't take quite enough.

Margaret Don't be such a bitch.

Laurie Well, I am.

Margaret You certainly make the same noises sometimes.

Laurie You're sure she didn't spend the weekend with our friend K. L.?

Margaret She was all on her own. I should have found out she was feeling like this. I'd have made her come with us.

Laurie Nice for us.

Margaret Leave her alone. There are some problems you've never had to face.

Laurie I should hope so.

The telephone in the sitting room rings. They stare at it.

Who the devil's that?

Margaret Well, you'd better answer it.

Laurie She hasn't told anyone else where we are?

Margaret No. No one. She hasn't spoken to anyone. Well, pick it up.

Annie does so.

Annie Room number . . . what's this one? Three-two-o. Yes . . . No . . . Just a moment. It's for Amy.

Laurie Amy!

Annie Amy! Phone! It's for you.

They wait. Amy appears, putting on her dressing gown.

Amy For me? How do they know?

Laurie I'll tell you.

Amy picks up the phone. Gillian appears in the doorway of Margaret's bedroom.

Amy (*on phone*) Hullo . . . Yes . . . Speaking . . . Oh, hullo, Paul. Yes . . . I see . . . No, wait a moment . . . Let me think . . . Their number's in a bright green leather book on his desk . . . Yes, in the study . . . No, I'll try and get a place earlier . . . No, don't do that . . . Stay there and I'll call you back. (*She puts the phone down.*) That was Paul. K. L.'s chauffeur . . . He's killed himself. He found him half an hour ago.

Pause. Dan comes in, in dressing gown.

Laurie How did he find the number?

Amy It was written on a pad by his desk. By his body.

Laurie starts to pour drinks for them all.

I suppose I'd better make some ticket arrangements.

Laurie Have a drink first. Here, sit down. Margaret.

Gus appears at his door.

Gus Annie? Hullo. I didn't hear someone on the phone, did I?

Annie K. L. has killed himself

Gus But how?

Amy Sleeping pills. Sleeping pills and aspirin.

Laurie Come in. Have a drink. You too, Gillian. Dan . . . Sleeping pills, aspirin, bottle of whisky, half a loaf of bread to keep it all down . . . give the housekeeper the weekend off, turn the extension off in your study and lock the front door . . . Well, cheers . . .

Silence.

Amy I think I'll talk to them downstairs from my room. Save you having to listen. I expect you'd all like to go back together if I can fix it?

Margaret Of course.

Dan I'll come with you. (*He follows her to their bedroom door. He says, a little drily:*) I wonder: if we'll ever come here again?

Margaret What – to this hotel?

Dan To Amsterdam . . .

Laurie I shouldn't think so. But I expect we might go somewhere else . . .

Dan closes his bedroom door. Curtain.